Cultural Diversity in the Workplace

Cultural Diversity in the Workplace

SALLY J. WALTON

Business Skills Express Series

IRWIN
Professional Publishing

MIRROR PRESS

Burr Ridge, Illinois
New York, New York
Boston, Massachusetts

Mirror Press:	David R. Helmstadter
	Carla F. Tishler
Editor-in-chief:	Jeffrey A. Krames
Project editor:	Amy E. Lund
Production manager:	Diane Palmer
Interior designer:	Jeanne M. Rivera
Cover designer:	Tim Kaage
Art manager:	Kim Meriwether
Compositor:	Alexander Graphics
Typeface:	12/14 Criterion
Printer:	Malloy Lithographing, Inc.

Library of Congress Cataloging-in-Publication Data

Walton, Sally J.
    Cultural diversity in the workplace / Sally J. Walton.
       p.   cm. — (The Business skills express series)
    ISBN 0-7863-0125-2
      1. Minorities—Employment—United States.   2. Multiculturalism—
United States.   3. Personnel management—United States.   I. Title.
II. Series.
    HF5549.5.M5W34   1994
    658.3'041—dc20   93–33174

Printed in the United States of America
2 3 4 5 6 7 8 9 0 ML 0 9 8 7 6 5 4

PREFACE

Trend toward Diversity

American culture is becoming increasingly diverse. It is no longer a melting pot, where new ethnic groups attempt to leave their original culture and language behind them. A more accurate image is a tossed salad, where various ingredients remain distinct even as they are mixed together.

Cultural diversity in the work environment will likely lead to changes in managerial style, employee negotiations, and motivating techniques. Techniques and strategies that work well with one group of employees may be ineffective or even insulting to another.

Workforce 2000

According to the US Department of Labor, the number of white males in the labor force will drop to 39.4 percent by the year 2000, down from 48.9 percent in 1976. More than 72 percent of new entrants into the workforce are women and minorities, and more than half of the already existing US workforce are women and minorities. White males currently make up only 45 percent of America's workforce, so it is this group that will be most pressed to change attitudes and behaviors.

In March 1991, the US Census Bureau released figures from its 1990 national census. During the last decade, the Asian-American population has more than doubled, and the Hispanic population has grown by 53 percent. Caucasians continue to decline as a proportion of the population, with only 6 percent growth, while the number of African-Americans has increased by 13 percent and Native Americans (American Indians) by 37.9 percent. More than a third of the nation's growth during the decade of the 1980s, from nearly 227 million to almost 249 million, came from immigration. That growth, primarily from Asians and Hispanics, is for the first time reflected in all regions of the country.

Cultural Diversity Is an Advantage in the Workplace

Managing cultural diversity effectively is a skill that can be learned. The key is realizing that cultural diversity is an *advantage* in the workplace. Diverse points of view, cultural orientations, insights, and perspectives breathe new life into your business. Strategies for marketing, sales, negotiation, or whatever other operations your organization is involved in or has targeted for the future will be enhanced by your ability to encourage and utilize diverse perspectives.

Is your customer base even more diverse than your workforce? Think about the advantage of having diversity in your workforce offering different points of view, approaches, and perspectives valuable to the success and acceptance of your products or services.

Here are some of the advantages of the organization that values its diverse workforce:

- In-house diversity gives insight to wider international markets.
- Innovative product design can come from listening to points of view different from your own.
- More astute marketing strategies can come from diverse perspectives.
- Better customer service is offered by a diverse workforce that reflects and understands the differing needs and preferences of those who make up your customer or client bases.
- Access to a wider talent pool.
- Opportunity to develop overlooked talent.

Valuing cultural diversity is clearly the way to keep your business competitive and productive.

Sally J. Walton

ABOUT THE AUTHOR

Sally J. Walton has nearly 15 years of international experience. She has lived in three very different cultures and has worked in or visited 38 countries. Her work as a professional speaker, consultant, seminar leader, and author focuses on maximizing human performance with a global perspective.

In pioneering and managing projects involving 25 nationalities, Ms. Walton has cultivated expertise in successfully communicating and getting results. Currently based in Santa Cruz, California, Ms. Walton serves clients nationally and internationally.

ABOUT IRWIN PROFESSIONAL PUBLISHING

Irwin Professional Publishing is the nation's premier publisher of business books. As a Times Mirror company, we work closely with Times Mirror training organizations, including Zenger-Miller, Inc., Learning International, Inc., and Kaset International to serve the training needs of business and industry.

About the Business Skills Express Series

This expanding series of authoritative, concise, and fast-paced books delivers high-quality training on key business topics at a remarkably affordable cost. The series will help managers, supervisors and frontline personnel in organizations of all sizes and types hone their business skills while enhancing job performance and career satisfaction.

Business Skills Express books are ideal for employee seminars, independent self-study, on-the-job training, and classroom-based instruction. Express books are also convenient-to-use references at work.

CONTENTS

Self-Assessment

How do you feel about your present knowledge and understanding of cultural diversity in the workplace? The following self-assessment will point to current strengths, as well as areas where you need improvement, as you begin *Cultural Diversity in the Workplace.*

	Almost Always	Sometimes	Almost Never
1. I am completely comfortable with cultural diversity in my current workplace.	_____	_____	_____
2. I am familiar with my colleagues' cultural backgrounds and traditions.	_____	_____	_____
3. I communicate effectively with people from different backgrounds.	_____	_____	_____
4. I understand the role of gender in relationship to management style.	_____	_____	_____
5. I build mentoring relationships at work.	_____	_____	_____
6. I can work well in diverse teams to solve problems.	_____	_____	_____
7. I avoid stereotyping my employees or colleagues.	_____	_____	_____
8. I clearly communicate expectations.	_____	_____	_____
9. I plan performance evaluations with a sensitivity to diversity.	_____	_____	_____
10. I understand the interaction between individual culture and organizational culture.	_____	_____	_____

1 | You're Already an Expert

This chapter will help you to:

- Define your culture.
- Be aware of the many elements that form our view of the world.
- Discover that these elements also form our values.

Generally, until human beings have the opportunity to learn otherwise, they assume that other people look at the world just as they do, everyone has similar values, and everyone is motivated for the same reasons.

How would you describe some of your own assumptions about values? That's a difficult task because we don't see assumptions. We think that's just the way the world is.

Values and behaviors that we've absorbed since childhood reflect differences in societal values and behaviors based on how and where we grew up. Some factors that affect these differences are:

- What country you were born in, what region within that country, what city—urban or rural—within that region, and what neighborhood within that city.
- Family values and behaviors in the home, which are influenced by religious beliefs, race, gender, socioeconomic (class and financial) considerations, and education.
- Individual personalities and idiosyncrasies.

Which of these factors had the biggest impact on your values?

_____

_____

_____

YOUR EXPERIENCE WITH CULTURAL DIVERSITY

Remember the story about the city mouse and the country mouse? In each of our lives, we have had similar experiences. We like what we're used to because we grew up with it. For most people, what we know is more comfortable than what we don't know.

Think about the times you moved from:

- A small town to a big city, or vice versa.
- One geographical region to another.
- Single to being married, or vice versa.
- Home to school or to your first apartment.
- School to first job.

What are some of the major behavior changes you experienced?

_____

_____

_____

With each of these changes, you've encountered a change of cultures and shifted your own behavior (slightly or dramatically) in order to function effectively in the new culture. Any change of geographical location, religion, marital status, or job, has given you experience in cultural diversity and has likely affected your values as well.

What are some of the things you've learned?

_____

_____

In addition to these major changes, you continue to make cultural shifts in your daily life as you go home to visit family, get involved in a new hobby, or even learn new jargon in order to make an intelligent purchase of a new piece of electronic equipment (stereo, fax machine, etc.).

What behavior shifts do you make daily as you shift from work to home or among different clients or customers?

_____

_____

Look at your list. Those behavior shifts and shifts of perception mean that you already have experience with cultural diversity. You can use that small-scale experience when you encounter cultural diversity in broader forms. Just as you shift perspective and behavior in the situation described above, you also do this when you interact with people of different ages, ethnic groups, nationalities, and so on.

DEFINING YOUR OWN CULTURE

How do you define your own cultural group? Do you define yourself first in terms of your nationality, ethnicity, race, religion, gender, age group, or other category of cultural diversity? List your categories here:

_____

_____

_____

Write the first three words that come to your mind about your own cultural group.

1. _____

2. _____

3. _____

Look at the list you've just written. Do you think someone outside your cultural group would choose the same words to describe your cultural group?

Now write the first three words that come to your mind about cultural groups with which you are working.

1. _____

2. _____

3. _____

List at least four of your concerns and four of your expectations in working together with the cultural groups you just listed above.

Concerns

1. _____

2. _____

3. _____

4. _____

Expectations

1. _____

2. _____

3. _____

4. _____

Do the lists you've just made reflect certain values? What are they?

_____

_____

_____

Look at your lists once again. How did your ideas about your own culture or another culture get formed?

_____

_____

_____

In the next chapter, we'll look further at the interaction between values, cultural groups, and culture. Now that you've begun to assess and define your own culture, you have the basis to think about culture in broader terms—the first step toward making the most of cultural diversity in the workplace.

Chapter 1 Checkpoints

✓ Each change in your life has given you an experience of a new culture.

✓ Be aware of the small way you experience cultural diversity almost every day.

✓ Realize that your perceptions of your own cultural group may not be the same as other people's perceptions of you, and vice versa.

2 | What Is Culture?

This chapter will help you to:

- Understand how culture affects your perceptions.
- See that values are on a spectrum.
- Explore your position on each of the value ranges.

WHAT IS CULTURE?

Whenever a group of people spend a period of time together, a culture is formed. Culture is a pattern of values and beliefs reflected in outer behaviors. The values supporting those outer behaviors are a key to understanding cultural differences.

■ Cultural Self-Awareness

A good place to start understanding cultural values is to know what your own basic values are. List at least three of your personal values that were instilled by the person most influential in your developmental years. (This person could be a parent, grandparent, teacher, or friend.)

1. _____

2. _____

3. _____

Culture is shaped by these lasting values that you're given at an early age. Can you think of ways these values are expressed in your life? (Some examples could be when you've faced difficult decisions or when you've made lifestyle choices.)

2

1. _____

2. _____

3. _____

Any culture that is formed over time by a group of people has accepted behaviors, expected behaviors, and, eventually, traditions. This is true also in our organizations, which is why we use the term *corporate culture*. Now let's move from your personal values to the values reflected in your workplace. In corporate life:

What traits do you value in your subordinates?

_____

_____

_____

What traits do you think your subordinates value in you?

_____

_____

_____

What does it take to succeed in your organization?

_____

_____

_____

Look at the lists you've just created. Do you think they reflect a set of cultural values and assumptions? How would you describe those values and assumptions?

_____

_____

_____

You've been discovering what causes particular values to be formed, and what values are central to your life and your workplace. Now we're going to expand that understanding to show how values are part of a spectrum.

Remember all the elements that influence your values. If these elements were arranged differently, they could result in a very different set of values, especially if reinforced by a large group of people. In other words, if you had grown up in a different culture, your values might be different.

The values chart that follows can show your values in relation to values commonly held throughout the world. Be aware that there is no right or wrong position on the scale of values. As you've seen, individuals in any group will vary in values and beliefs—there is no top or bottom to a values spectrum. Spectrums show a continuum rather than fixed movement from left to right or good to bad.

CULTURAL VALUES SPECTRUM*

Control	Fate
Individual	Group
Change	Stability
Self-Made	Birthright
Equality	Hierarchy
Time	Human Interaction
Competition	Cooperation
Future	Past
Doing	Being
Informality	Formality
Direct	Indirect
Practicality	Idealism
Material	Spiritual

For each of the spectrums (marked by a ▪) on pages 9 through 18, we'll define both poles. Where do you find your own values along each spectrum? Consider where other cultural groups' values might fall along each spectrum. How could differences in these values impact the workplace?

■ Control_____Fate

Personal control over the environment:

- It is normal and right for humans to control nature.
- Individuals control their own environment and lives.

_____

*Adapted from L Robert Kohls.

Fate or destiny:

- Some things lie beyond the power of humans.

Americans are more oriented toward the control end of the spectrum. We tend to believe in the capacity and responsibility of people to take control of their own lives and circumstances. In other cultures, people may feel that job promotions, transfers, and success are more in the hands of fate or the will of a supreme being.

Americans also tend to believe that it is normal and right to control nature and the environment. At the other end of the spectrum is the belief that some things lie beyond the power of humans.

Where do you think people from other cultural groups might be along the control/fate spectrum?

_____

_____

How does this influence your behavior when working with people from other cultural groups?

_____

_____

Individual_____Group

Individualism:

- Each individual is unique and special.
- Privacy is a positive and desired condition.
- Independence is valued.

Group orientation:

- Strong identification with group.
- Privacy may connote loneliness or isolation.
- Dependence is normal.

The dominant American culture is individualistic. Each person is viewed as unique and special. People are expected to be independent and to do things for themselves. Privacy is a positive and desired condition.

2

At the other end of this spectrum are cultures that place a high value on the group. This is expressed as loyalty to, identification with, and responsibility for the extended family or work team. Privacy may be an unknown or little-understood concept.

Place a mark where you think you are along the individual/group spectrum of values. How would your position affect working with others who are positioned differently on the spectrum?

_____

_____

◼ Change_____Stability

Change is a good and positive condition:

- It is linked to development, improvement, progress, and growth.
- It is seen as natural.

Change is disruptive:

- It is a destructive force to be avoided.
- Stability, continuity, tradition, and ancient heritage are valued.

In cultures emphasizing the individual, change is usually seen as positive. Mobility is a sign of independence and progress. Changing homes, jobs, or even spouses is often linked to growth and improvement.

Such change is viewed as natural in mainstream American culture, but it can be confusing to cultures that value maintaining close family ties, or working for one company for life. For people with these values, the preference is for stability, continuity, and tradition.

Place a mark where you think you are along the change/stability spectrum of values. How do you think possessing different values and attitudes would affect groups or individuals working together?

_____

_____

■ Self-Made_____Birthright

Accomplishment decides condition of life:

- Condition of birth is not credited.
- Hard work and sacrifice are keys to success.
- Take the initiative.

Family background decides condition of life:

- Individual accomplishment is within context of birthright.
- Inheritance is a major factor.

The self-made/birthright continuum is related to both the individual/group and control/fate spectrums. Self-made societies value the accomplishments of the individual. Hard work and sacrifice are keys to success. Value is assigned to the person taking initiative, not to the condition of one's birth. In the United States, heroes overcome humble beginnings to become wealthy or overcome birth in a log cabin to become president.

In contrast some cultures believe strongly that family background and inheritance decide the lifelong condition of a person's life. In these cultures, individual accomplishment can only be felt within the context of one's birth.

Where do you place yourself along the self-made/birthright spectrum of values?

_____

_____

How might a viewpoint different from yours be expressed?

_____

_____

■ Equality_____Hierarchy

Equality is valued as a right:

- All people are created equal.
- All people have an equal opportunity to succeed in life.
- All people are treated just like everyone else.

Rank, status, and authority are desirable:

- They give a sense of security and certainty.
- It is reassuring to know who and where one is in society.
- People are treated differently according to their status.

For people who value equality, it is difficult to imagine preferring classifications that clearly differentiate groups. Yet these allow a security of knowing one's place, expected behavior, dress, and so on.

Place a mark where you think you are along the equality/hierarchy spectrum of values. How would different backgrounds in relation to this spectrum affect behavior in the workplace?

_____

_____

■ Time_____Human Interaction

Time is of utmost importance:

- Concern with schedules is of high priority.
- Language is filled with references to time.

Relationships are more important than schedules:

- Abruptly cutting off a discussion is worse than being late.

Possibly no other spectrum has more impact on the success or failure of working relationships than this one. Differing views of time and its use are key sources of frustration in working together. For many people, human interaction is a major factor in their decision to do business with you or an organization.

Where are you along the time/human interaction spectrum of values? What about others from different cultural groups?

_____

_____

How do these positions influence your behavior when working with people from different cultural groups?

_____

_____

Competition_____Cooperation

Competition brings out the best:

- In the classroom, work, and sports.
- Every individual is competing with all others.

Cooperation leads to the best results:

- Team spirit and group effort are most important.

This spectrum is a good example of how changes in management and corporate values can produce the best results in a business environment. In the United States, competition among individuals within a company is shifting toward emphasis on teams and group effort.

Where are you along the competition/cooperation spectrum of values? Where is your organization?

_____

_____

How does this affect different cultural groups when working together?

_____

_____

■ Future_____Past

The future will bring improvement and greater happiness:

- Energy is directed toward the future.
- Planning for the future is important.

Orientation to past:

- Remembering the past is important.
- Planning for the future is futile or even sinful.

The United States generally is a very future-focused nation. Rather than having a long past history, this country was formed by those seeking a brighter future. On the other hand, you may encounter co-workers who come from a country with a rich history that spans centuries.

Where are you on the future/past spectrum of values? What cultural groups may have a stronger orientation toward the past than yours does?

_____

_____

How would this influence your working with people from these groups?

_____

_____

■ Doing_____Being

Action orientation:

- Work is primary.
- Plan full schedules.
- Leisure activities (recreation) are only to *re-create* ability to work hard.

Just being has value and gives value:

- Hard work, especially physical labor, may not be prized.

Not only will you find that places along this spectrum differ by nationality, but also that they differ by region.

Where are you along the doing/being spectrum of values? What differences have you encountered with people from different cultural groups, including different regions of your own country?

_____

_____

How does this influence your working together?

_____

_____

■ Informality_____Formality

Informality is valued:

- Dress is casual.
- Individuals are called by their first names.
- Greetings are short.

Formality maintains stability in society:

- Dress is according to status.
- Individuals are addressed by their titles.
- Greetings are respectful.

This spectrum goes much deeper than the etiquette of formality in dress. How people are addressed, how meetings are run, and who has lunch together are all affected by this spectrum.

Where are you along the informality/formality spectrum of values? What about others in your workplace and the general corporate culture?

_____

_____

How does this influence your behavior in working together?

_____

_____

■ Direct_____Indirect

Directness:

- Evaluations are short and succinct, even when negative.
- Honesty and openness are valued.
- Use of an intermediary is seen as manipulative.

Subtleness:

- Ritualistic ways of giving bad news are used.
- Saving face is important.
- Use of an intermediary may preserve harmony.

Individuals and organizations in the United States are realizing that "putting all your cards on the table," "getting it off your chest," or "telling how you *really* feel" is not universally regarded as positive or appropriate behavior.

Where are you along the direct/indirect spectrum of values? What about others from different cultural groups?

_____

_____

In what situations could these positions cause problems in your organization?

_____

_____

■ Practicality_____Idealism

Practical considerations are given high priority:

- Efficiency is a source of pride.
- Individuals control their own environments and lives.

Theory is valued:

- Subjective and emotional ideals have a place.

Groups and individuals have varying comfort levels with theoretical versus practical approaches. In the workplace, be aware that the preference for discussing, sometimes emotionally, all the reasons and options in a proposal can have cultural roots. A "let's just try a few and see what works" approach is at the other end of the spectrum.

Where are you along the practicality/idealism spectrum of values? What about others from different cultural groups?

_____

_____

How does this influence your behavior when working with people from those groups?

_____

_____

◼ Material_____Spiritual

Materialism is a natural benefit of hard work:

- Acquiring objects is a prime motivator in life.
- Individuals give high priority to obtaining, maintaining, and protecting their material objects.

Detachment from material objects is a value:

- The meaning of life is found in the realm of the spirit.

Differences along this spectrum are reflected in everything from home furnishing styles to use of time. In the workplace, one's position on the spectrum can affect motivation and communication.

Where would you place yourself along the material/spiritual spectrum of values? What about others from different cultural groups?

_____

_____

How might this influence your behavior when working with people from those groups?

_____

_____

As you can see, culture is made up of the interactions of all these values and others. In this chapter, you've seen that culture is not static or rigid but more flowing and variable. The general, shared values of a group determine culture, but even these general beliefs can change over time and within the context of environment.

2

Chapter 2 Checkpoints

✓ Culture is shaped by values that we're given at an early age.

✓ Traits valued in your workplace are reflective of a set of cultural values and assumptions.

✓ Values are on a spectrum, reflecting different ways in which people look at the world.

3 | Cultural Diversity at Work

This chapter will help you to:

- See each individual as a culture of one.
- Understand that stereotypes can prevent clear vision.
- See how assumptions based on stereotypes can fog work effectiveness.

EVERYONE IS A CULTURAL GROUP OF ONE

When we speak of cultural diversity in the workplace, we're not just speaking of nationalities or ethnic groups, but also of age, gender, race, religion, sexual orientation, physical abilities, where you live (metropolitan/small town/rural locations), plus subcultures within any of these categories based on occupation, education, and personality.

Culture is formed by all the elements that we looked at in the first two chapters: where you were born, family values, religious beliefs, race, gender, socioeconomic factors, education, and personality. The combination of elements makes each individual unique.

All groups and cultures are much too complex for one-stereotype-fits-all assumptions. In your organization a winning attitude is to assume that everyone is a cultural group of one. That way you'll be seeing individuals for what they can handle and how they can grow rather than seeing only your assumptions about them.

STEREOTYPES

Stereotypes can be useful in alerting you to broad areas of uniqueness (e.g., Europeans generally are more formal than Americans), although even these generalizations may often be suspect. Stereotypes are of limited value, however, when interacting with one individual. They can limit the way you see a person's true talents, ambitions, and preferences.

This can happen quickly, easily, and subconsiously. Your brain recognizes, "This is a black woman, an older person, a Native American, someone who doesn't speak English well, a white male." Depending on your stereotypes, you could be missing what that person is saying, wanting, or capable of doing.

Let's imagine for a moment that there are two girls who grew up in the same era, same town, same ethnic group, and, in fact, next door to each other. One family thought it was OK for a girl to go into business and encouraged it. The other family thought a girl should be a nurse, secretary, or homemaker. Would those girls of the same age, same region, and same ethnic group have similar personalities, values, and abilities? What might be some of their differences?

_____

_____

_____

Even positive stereotypes pigeonhole people and their abilities and don't allow managers to effectively use the talents of employees. If you think older workers are conservative, you may not hear an innovative idea from an older worker.

When you find yourself choosing one person over another for a task, ask yourself if you have assumptions about both of their capabilities. Think back to Chapter 1 and how you form your assumptions. Notice the assumptions you have about people at work. Were they formed from actual performance at work, from one or two encounters with someone of that culture outside of work, or even from a movie? What are some of the factors forming your assumptions about others?

_____

_____

_____

■ Assigning Characteristics

This activity will make you more aware of your responses to stereotypes. Note what you think about the people you meet during the day—either at work or just passing on the street. For example, what kinds of stereotypes come to mind when you see a female executive, an African-American male, an Asian child, an older woman, or an older man?

_____

_____

_____

_____

Do you think your initial responses are preventing you from exploring the talents of each person?

_____

_____

■ Perception of Cultures

Remember that white males are a numerical minority since they make up only 45 percent of America's workforce. However, the dominant environment of American organizational life continues, for the most part, to be one that was formed by white males. What have you experienced as rules of white male corporate culture?

_____

_____

_____

_____

The following characteristics may be examples of white male corporate culture:

- Action is valued more than deliberation.
- Reason is valued more than intuition.
- Leading is valued more than asking.
- Business is a battlefield in which combatants aren't supposed to take things personally.

How do individuals you know deal with the workplace environment based on these rules? For many women and minorities, following these rules doesn't come easily. For example, they often find that the lack of relationships necessary to further their careers or get the information they need is an obstacle.

Business as Usual

List a few of the organizational roles in your workplace. (Some examples might be CEO, accountant, receptionist, line supervisor, or new employee.)

_____

_____

_____

_____

Write down your description of the people or types of people who are in these organizational roles in your workplace.

_____

_____

_____

Ask yourself this question: Do you respond to the people in these roles differently if they are male or female; older or younger; Asian-American, African-American, or European-American? In any organization there are roles, and there are often assumptions (gender, age, etc.) about what type of person should fill those roles. These assumptions regarding roles in the workplace do shift over time. One example is the returning prevalence of male secretaries.

Watching Films in a New Way

A good time to practice your new awareness in communicating through the filters of cultural diversity is while watching films. As you watch, note different communication styles and expectations. After any current or classic film you watch, ask yourself the questions on page 25.

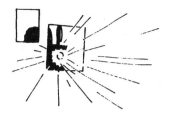

3

What stereotypes are reinforced or negated in the film?

_____
_____
_____
_____

Where did communication break down, and why?

_____
_____
_____
_____

Have you had similar experiences in your own life?

_____
_____
_____
_____

How did you deal with the situations? What would you do differently?

_____
_____
_____
_____

Although life doesn't always imitate art, you probably have seen communication problems in the workplace too. In Chapter 4, we'll look at ways to bridge cultural gaps in communication styles.

3

Chapter 3 Checkpoints

✓ Assume that everyone in your organization is a culture of one.

✓ There are usually unwritten rules in an organization.

✓ These rules are often obstacles for those who don't know or understand them.

✓ Roles in an organization are often associated with particular ages, genders, and ethnic groups.

CHAPTER

4

Communication and Improved Performance

This chapter will help you to:

- Discover that cultural filters are present in communication.
- Practice using open questions to help communication.

CULTURAL FILTERS

In Chapter 1 we looked at the many elements that make up culture. Those same elements influence your patterns of communication and how successfully you send or receive information. Imagine those elements as filters—communication looks something like the accompanying figure:

CULTURAL FILTERS

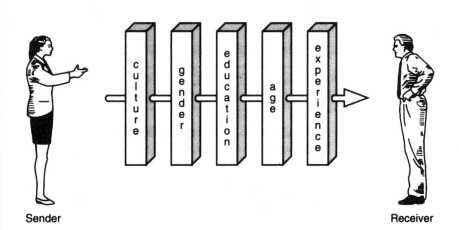

Sender   Receiver

Consider the following points:

- Communication between sender and receiver passes through filters of culture, age, gender, education, and experience.
- This often leads to misperceptions, misinterpretations, and misevaluations.
- Improved communication begins with awareness of these filters.

What examples are there from your own life where cultural filters impeded communication?

_____

_____

_____

_____

In many cultures, communication is more than just words; it involves the whole context of the encounter. The status of the individuals, the setting, body language, voice tone, and phrasing all contribute to the subtleties of what is communicated. The exchange of information is subordinate to building and maintaining the relationship.

Americans depend on verbal and linguistic communication. Asians, on the other hand, use nonverbal communication and innuendos to allow people to maintain their dignity in awkward situations.

What examples are there from your own life where age differences impeded communication? (For example, do you speak the same language as teenagers?)

_____

_____

_____

_____

Being born in a different country may cause communication challenges here, but even someone born in your own home may have a vocabulary and manner of communication different from yours, especially if there are age differences involved. So if your workplace includes people with generational differences, realize that you may encounter filters in communication.

Gender influences communication styles even within the same culture. For males of mainstream American culture, the object of a conversation, generally, is to give or receive information. Women of mainstream American culture, on the other hand, tend to communicate within the context of the relationship at hand, not simply to give or receive information.

How do gender differences in communication influence your behavior in working with members of the opposite sex?

_____

_____

_____

_____

4

ARE YOU COMMUNICATING EFFECTIVELY?

At work, you have to give direction and feedback. You can develop a more precise vocabulary to improve the effectiveness of your communication. First of all, consider whether your terminology is clear to everybody.

Take this page and, for the next several hours, note down the regional expressions or slang that you hear at work. If you notice this in your own speech, write down expressions that *you* use as well.

Jargon, insider jokes,* or slang that I've heard at work today:

_____

_____

_____

_____

Daily language is filled with clichés and slang so commonly used that we don't even think about whether we're understood. Do your colleagues know what you're talking about when you "up the ante," "deep-six a project," or "make an end run"?

As you "get all your ducks in a row," also be aware of the use of *acronyms*. People in some industries and agencies seem to talk in code with scarcely a word recognizable to outsiders.

---

*Insider jokes, or expressions, come about through shared experiences and can be totally baffling to someone who hasn't shared them. Worse, that person can feel left out, or even laughed *at*.

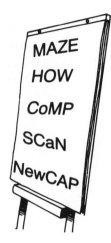

GETTING TO NO

When you use expressions or give explanations that others can't understand, don't assume that another person will tell you so. Recall the Direct_____Indirect spectrum of values. American culture has traditionally valued directness, but not all cultures do.

Some people will nod their heads yes and not ask questions, even if they don't understand. You've probably done this at some point in your life. Most of us have, so we don't appear "stupid," or because we don't want to take the time to hear the explanations again. However, in your workplace, there may be someone who doesn't ask questions in order to save *you* face. He or she may not want to give the impression that you are not being a good communicator!

What ideas do you have for avoiding this problem?

_____

_____

_____

_____

Open-Ended Questions

Perhaps your ideas include the use of open-ended questions. Using open-ended questions is a good strategy for any communication between people of different ages, genders, or nationalities.

A closed-ended question can be answered with yes or no, closing further discussion. Open-ended questions, on the other hand, open the possibility of elaboration and clarification.

Write a closed-ended question that you might use at work (e.g., "Can you do this by Thursday?").

_____

_____

Change that to an open-ended question (e.g., "Can you tell me how you will do this?").

4

> **Hint** ─────────────────────────────
>
> Begin open-ended questions with "who," "how," "why," "where," "when," "what," or "tell me."

_____

_____

TIPS FOR COMMUNICATING

Your communication is a form of coaching and staff development. This is helpful to remember if you feel hurried or frustrated. If you are working with employees who are non-native English speakers, here are a few basic tips:

- Speak clearly.
- Avoid slang expressions.
- Condense your communication to the main point.
- Refrain from extraneous explanations and elaboration; they can be confusing.
- Repeat your main point.
- Speak simply, but in correct English.
- Use a visual accompaniment or brief written note when appropriate.

- Note nonverbal clues of confusion rather than asking "Do you understand?"
- Communicate what you want done and how to do it to assist employee productivity.

Now that you understand the basics of communicating across cultural filters and see how cultures are based on shared values, it's time to consider how to effectively manage this diversity.

4

Chapter 4 Checkpoints

✓ Use open-ended questions.

✓ Be aware of jargon, slang, and insider references that impede understanding.

✓ Cultural filters directly affect the way messages are sent and received.

✓ Recognizing common filters, such as age, race, gender, and experience, is the first step in becoming a better communicator.

5 | Getting the People You Want

This chapter will help you to:

- Discover your picture of the ideal employee.
- See that this image may prevent you from finding the people you need.
- Learn interviewing skills that can breech cultural differences.

Some employers are finding that their first step in effectively managing a diverse workforce is to relinquish the image of an ideal employee as someone with a neat appearance who wants an eight-hour shift and is willing to work overtime. Basing your recruiting on your image of the ideal employee may bring few, if any, candidates to your door. The challenge is to attract, retain, and motivate *individuals* with very *diverse* characteristics. Diversity leads to a more interesting, innovative, and productive work environment—one that reflects the diverse American society at large.

THE IDEAL EMPLOYEE

What are your expectations and stereotypes of the ideal employee? Take 15 minutes to list what you consider an ideal employee. (If you are working in a group, you can do this exercise together on a flip chart.)

_____
_____
_____
_____
_____
_____

After you've created the list, go back and note, after each characteristic, whether or not you associate it with a certain type of person (e.g., with women, older workers, or Asians).

How does your preconception of an ideal employee and preconceptions of certain types or categories of people impact both hiring practices and the assignments that you entrust to your employees?

_____

_____

_____

_____

The following case study shows some of the pitfalls involved with having preconceptions of the ideal employee.

Blowing Your Own Horn Is Not a Universal Concept*

Bill Jenkenson interviewed applicants for two days without success. The résumé of Lily Mandaly, in front of him now, looked promising. She had excellent experience even though she had never worked in the United States. He was looking forward to hearing how Lily had achieved her accomplishments in her various positions, especially since she came with such good references.

When Lily came in, however, she did not project the dynamic go-getter that Bill had imagined from her résumé. Lily seemed bright and capable, but she looked down most of the time, which made Bill uncomfortable. He wondered if she could handle the tough assignments he needed covered.

Worse yet, when he asked her to talk about what she had contributed in her previous positions, she answered that the successes listed in her résumé had been the results of team efforts. Bill began to assume that she wasn't all that capable and that possibly she was even dishonest for listing accomplishments on her résumé that she was reluctant to brag about. ∎

---

*After reading this vignette, complete the worksheet that follows on page 39.

▪ **W o r k s h e e t**

1. How would *you* interpret Lily's actions and demeanor?

_____

_____

2. During the interview, how could Bill have gotten the information he needed?

_____

_____

3. What assumptions did Bill have about interview behavior?

_____

_____

4. If you had coached Lily to prepare for the interview, what would you have said?

_____

_____

5. Assume that Lily is of a minority population. What benefits do you see in hiring culturally diverse employees?

_____

_____

Points to Consider

How did your responses compare to the following guidelines? Notice the emphasis on communication style and the interplay of gender, culture, and values.

1. How would *you* interpret Lily's actions and demeanor?

- Recent immigrants are still learning the rules of their new culture. Assertive behavior, such as actively asking questions during the interview or offering additional information, may not be a positive value for them.
- Marketing oneself may be a totally new concept. Personality traits you have looked for before may prevent you from discovering the people you need, and thus you may lose talented candidates.
- Consider gender differences in communication styles. Women may tend to speak in tentative or questioning phrases to avoid appearing too aggressive and to avoid inviting dialogue and establishing a relationship with the interviewer, which they may feel is inappropriate.
- For the interviewee, especially if she is from a culture with great respect for authority, looking an interviewer straight in the eye may be a sign of disrespect.

2. During the interview, how could Bill have gotten the information he needed?

- It may be necessary to allow time to learn the individual's role and accomplishments, as she may not easily talk about herself in these terms.
- Time allowances also must be given for building a rapport in order for the interviewee to speak freely.
- Cultural emphasis on modesty may prevent an interviewee from listing or describing accomplishments or personal attributes.

- Ask about others involved in the same project and how the candidate viewed the accomplishment of the team. Then it's possible to ask how the other members or supervisor of the team would describe the interviewee's role. This allows a person uncomfortable with boasting to speak of his accomplishments indirectly.
- Consider having a culturally diverse team interview the candidate. Not only does this offer individual role models for the candidate but also makes a statement about the organization's commitment to diversity.

3. What assumptions did Bill have about interview behavior?

- For most interviewers, looking someone directly in the eye connotes honesty and attention, in other words, positive traits desirable in a new hire.
- During the interview, ask yourself, Is this happening because it is culturally appropriate for the other person to do it?
- Achieving a culturally diverse talent pool requires rethinking previous assumptions and methods in the selection process.

4. If you had coached Lily to prepare for the interview, what would you have said?

- Practice looking your interviewer directly in the eye; this connotes honesty and attention. Be ready to talk about your accomplishments, and actively ask questions concerning the job.

5. Assume that Lily is of a minority population. What benefits do you see in hiring culturally diverse employees?

- Cultural diversity in your organization offers advantages because your customer base is increasingly diverse.
- Look for high levels of commitment and motivation rather than prior experience. Often, recent immigrants, older workers, returning-to-work women, and disabled people are eager for the opportunity to demonstrate their trainability and capacity on the job. This diversity can give you the results you want.

5

Chapter 5 Checkpoints

✓ Your concept of an ideal employee may be preventing you from finding the talent you need.

✓ When you are puzzled about behavior, consider that it might result from cultural differences.

✓ Use questions about team accomplishments if interviewees seem reticent to speak about their own accomplishments.

6 | Mentoring, Age, and Authority

This chapter will help you to:

- Discover that mentoring is a key to productivity and success.
- Understand that mentoring is two-way learning.
- Understand differences in how age and authority are viewed in the workplace.

In the last chapter, you explored some of the ways to find good employees. In this chapter you will learn how to be more productive in the workplace through mentoring, coaching, and two-way learning.

The process of mentoring offers one of the best avenues for creating a collective organizational culture while demonstrating openness to individual and group differences. A combination of mentoring and training can result in valuable and effective employees.

MENTORING

Mentoring is helping another person access information and networks. It is coaching the employee to succeed and giving support to that process. Mentoring is two-way learning, especially when the mentoring relationship crosses ethnic, gender, racial, and other forms of diversity. State your willingness and desire for mentoring to go both ways. The mentoree is helping you, the mentor, understand how to better communicate with people who are different from you.

Communicate your organization's culture to new employees. Explain expected dress and behavior. Be sure that all members of the organization have the tools to succeed and to understand the special qualities of difference that each brings to the workplace.

6

Mentoring should:

- Help employees understand the expectations of the organization.
- Coach employees on how to develop the skills necessary for their jobs.
- Give the encouragement for them to do so.
- Offer training to provide employees opportunities to practice new skills.
- Share access to information and networks.

Let's go back to the point that your communication is a form of coaching and staff development. You are building communication skills. You are aware of obstacles to effective communication and are honing your skill in reducing those obstacles. Now you have a chance to practice even more, with the following situation. Read the case study and then consider the questions that come after it.

Yes?

After a rousing meeting to increase sales of retail ads, Catherine Donnelly went up to one of the newest recruits, Jay.

Catherine

"Jay, I expect you to sell 45 ads by the end of the month."

Recruit

"Yes ma'am."

Catherine

"So, do I have your promise that you'll bring in 45 ads?"

Recruit

"Yes, ma'am."

Catherine

"Good, then you'll be joining the ranks of our best producers."

At the end of the month, Jay was nowhere near the goal that Catherine had asked of him and he had promised to deliver. Catherine was upset because she thought Jay should have come right out and told her that he wouldn't be able to sell so many ads. ■

1. What cultural factors may be involved in this situation?

_____

_____

_____

2. How could Catherine have assisted Jay in either setting a more realistic goal or in achieving the one called for?

_____

_____

_____

Points to Consider

- Jay feels that he is maintaining harmony in the situation by not questioning Catherine's expectations.

- In many minority cultures, one does not question or discuss the expectations of a supervisor. Mutual discussion or setting goals with an authority figure is not a common procedure. If an authority figure (boss, manager, or supervisor) asks for something to be done, the employee says yes whether or not it is possible to accomplish the task within the expected time frame.

- For some cultures, saying yes simply means "I hear what you're saying" rather than "I agree" or "I'll do it."

- To avoid the conflict between what one culture sees as honesty and another sees as disruption to harmony, Catherine and other supervisors can follow some general guidelines:

- Be aware that such differences exist and that there are valid underlying cultural values in both ways of looking at the situation.

- Avoid questions that call for yes or no answers.

- Ask open-ended questions like "What will you do to sell 45 ads by the end of the month?" "What actions will you take?" "How can I assist you in meeting this goal?" The response will indicate where coaching is needed for improved performance.

- There may be confusion about expectations or how to achieve these expectations, and embarrassment to admit it may result. The confusion may be due to terminology or lack of experience.

- Catherine's job is to make sure that Jay and others know how to go about increasing sales of retail ads. Have employees explain their strategies. Assess and add to those strategies or tactics.

- Even if the employee has a previously successful track record, the ways your company measures achievement may be different from the employee's previous situation.

- Catherine thought she was motivating Jay by saying that he would join the ranks of top producers, but a call for team effort may have been a more effective motivation in this case.

What other ideas do you have?

_____

_____

_____

AGE

In many cultures, age and authority are aligned. Traditionally, age brings positions of authority and respect; people in positions of authority are usually older.

Most non-native American employees have the respect for age ingrained as a cultural value. This means an older employee, even if not one with the most seniority, will have the respect of the group, perhaps even being an informal group leader.

What other kinds of behavior could result from giving high respect to people of older ages?

_____

_____

_____

An example could be some groups will find it difficult to work for a younger manager—the younger manager, must gain respect and authority. How would you go about this?

_____

_____

_____

_____

Here are some suggestions:

- Find out the expressions of respect in that particular culture, and show overt respect to the older members of the group. Showing respect to those you are supervising may mean addressing them as Mr./Ms. _____ or learning a respectful prefix or suffix from their culture. Your attitude will go a long way toward overcoming resistance or discomfort.

- Promoting a younger member of the group before an older person can also cause difficulties, or even resignations. It is possible to deal with this situation by having the older person make the announcement to the group, and stating in private to both the younger person and the older person that you don't want either to lose face. Being aware of the possible reactions and letting employees know you are concerned goes a long way toward avoiding unwanted responses. An added plus is that the members of the group may offer a solution or approach that you have not thought of.

AUTHORITY ROLES

Some value systems teach great respect for, even fear of, authority.

It is extremely difficult for some employees to give feedback or input, since this means questioning the authority of their supervisor.

What kinds of behavior could result from giving high respect to authority figures?

_____

_____

_____

_____

Some examples could be:

- Inappropriate behavior from a supervisor may not be reported.
- An individual may resign rather than confront or criticize someone in a higher-authority position.

Most foreign-born employees respect authority. This respect may show itself by the employee's waiting to be told what to do and, consequently, seeming to lack initiative. An employee with this background may not question or disagree with a supervisor. If you don't understand the importance of authority roles in other cultures, you may think your employees are uninterested or unmotivated when they are really being respectful.

6

Chapter 6 Checkpoints

✓ Mentoring is two-way learning.

✓ While coaching new employees on expectations of your organization, you can learn from your mentorees more effective ways to work with different groups of people.

✓ Some cultures' respect for age and authority may result in a workplace different from what you're used to.

7 | Make Differences Work

> **This chapter will help you to:**
> - Take time to build relationships.
> - Use teamwork for improved morale and productivity.
> - See the influence of gender on management style.

All activities in an organization, including managing, training, appraisal, and recognition, will be enhanced by tailoring them to the individual. In an organization diverse in age, gender, ethnicity, and religion, fairness is not sameness. Individuals will have needs and motivations unique to their situation.

The rule for effectively managing cultural diversity is not "Do unto others as you would have others do unto you." Rather, it is "Do unto others as they would be done unto."

Each organization has its own personality or corporate culture. The art of leading a successful organization is to create an atmosphere where members of the organization enthusiastically support the collective mission and strategies.

Enthusiasm and loyalty aren't nurtured by force. Only in an environment where individuals feel valued, challenged, and recognized will participation move from a job-for-money to commitment.

RELATIONSHIPS

In the values spectrum of time and human interaction, you saw that interaction can have a higher value than time schedules in some cultures. In Asian, Middle Eastern, and Latin American cultures, relationship is of primary importance. Employees from these cultures often feel that they cannot approach an American manager unless there is a problem. Effective managers will allow time to interact with employees other than when giving orders or dealing with problems and crises.

Though relationships are extremely important, this should not translate into being overly friendly. Being too friendly right away may be inappropriate to people from more formal cultures. Instead, building a relationship refers more to the time given to establishing an environment of trust.

People from other cultures may take time to establish and reestablish relationships and may do this before each meeting. So while you may fret over delays to getting down to business, others may not understand why you don't take time for friendly chatting when you all come together. Being assertive may not be the only way to get a job done. Persistence or good relationships may achieve more with some cultures than assertiveness.

PERFORMANCE IMPROVEMENT THROUGH TEAMWORK

Given the importance that good relationships and the group have within many cultures, look to strategies that increase teamwork in order to improve performance. Ask yourself these questions:

Does your organization reflect shared values or are you all pulling in different directions?

_____

_____

_____

Do your employees recruit new talent and act as though the company were truly their own?

_____

_____

_____

Does your reward and recognition system motivate employees and reflect the vision of the company?

_____

_____

_____

How's the spirit in your organization?

_____

_____

_____

Celebrations

Celebrations improve teamwork and the spirit of the organization. Acknowledge a new account, birthdays, anniversaries of years with the company, or a special date or event in the history of the organization.

Festivities celebrate the organizational culture and all the individuals whose diversity contributes to it. Include observance of the holidays or family traditions of the countries represented by the diverse employees in your workplace. Inviting family members adds to the inclusiveness of the collective culture.

What other ideas do you have?

_____

_____

_____

TEAMWORK

The foundations for teamwork in a culturally diverse group are as follows:

- Personal awareness of values and operating styles.
- Finding or inventing ways to collaborate.
- Support for this process from the organization.

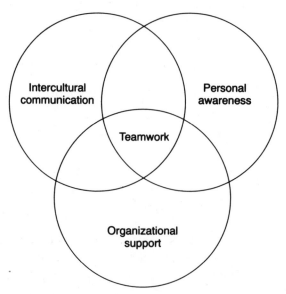

Teamwork is the result of communication, awareness, and support.

In your current work situation, what practical steps can you take to improve teamwork?

_____

_____

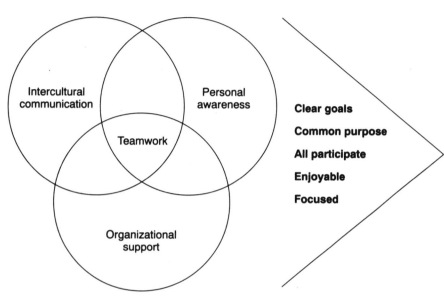

Teamwork leads to greater efficiency, productivity, and overall morale.

In your focus on improving teamwork in your workplace, how do you rate yourself on the following personal qualities that help form effective teams? Fill in S if you feel you rate satisfactorily. Fill in NI if you feel you need improvement.

An ability to listen to and respect other points of view _____.

Intellectual curiosity and a positive attitude toward new experiences _____.

Willingness to take risks _____.

Sense of humor _____.

A high energy level _____.

Read the situation that follows and answer the questions that follow.

7

You're the Best!

At the meeting to announce the winner of the sales contest, Catherine Donnelly called up Laura as the number one producer of retail ads for the paper. "You're the best!" Catherine announced.

To Catherine's surprise, Laura seemed embarrassed and simply mumbled, "We all worked hard as a team."

Even more surprising to Catherine, morale and sales of ads dropped somewhat after the contest. She had used the sales contest to motivate better performance and invested a lot in the prize. Where had she gone wrong? ■

1. What cultural factors may be involved in this situation?

_____

_____

2. What motivational strategies could Catherine have used to improve performance?

_____

_____

Points to Consider

- Shifting her perspective to the importance of the group over the individual would help Catherine successfully manage and motivate in a multicultural environment.
- In many cultures, the group will often assume responsibility for increased productivity and quality; the individual will want to contribute to the team's success rather than stand out alone.
- For motivation and reward systems, encouraging competition among individuals in some cultural groups is counterproductive.
- If only one person can win the prize or incentive, team spirit lags and some employees will be reluctant to sacrifice group solidarity for individual recognition. Better to capitalize on that group solidarity by fostering team spirit, team recognition, and reward.
- American-born women will have the societal values of individualism and competition but are more likely than their male counterparts to acknowledge members of the team that contributed to their success.

- The above behaviors are tendencies in these groups; there will always be exceptions. Individual preferences and idiosyncrasies are present in *all* cultures.

GENDER DIFFERENCES IN MANAGEMENT STYLE

Women brought up in mainstream American culture tend to have different styles of leadership and management than their male counterparts. Whereas men view their roles with employees as a series of transactions, women tend to build one-on-one and group relationships through ongoing collaboration.

- In resolving conflict or generating new ideas, women tend to listen to what others have to say rather than making unilateral decisions. This can be a plus in working in a diverse workplace.
- There's a special challenge, however, when a woman is supervising members of a cultural group in which women do not have leadership positions over men. Here, again, the learning must go both ways: Show respect and understanding while demonstrating your authority and capability.
- When women are supervising or are peers with men of the same ethnic or national background, challenges can be more acute. Examples in the United States would be the difficulties of women who have entered the traditionally male-dominated fields of manufacturing, trucking, and firefighting.

If you are a woman and a manager, you may already have the relationship and communication skills that foster teamwork in a diverse environment. In Chapters 8 and 9, we'll discuss how men *and* woman can use these skills in two common tasks: performance evaluations and conflict resolution.

Chapter 7 Checkpoints

✓ Building relationships is a key to success in a culturally diverse workplace.

✓ Treat people as *they* prefer to be treated.

✓ Teamwork fosters a sense of loyalty to the organization and can increase productivity as well as morale.

8 | Performance Evaluation

> **This chapter will help you to:**
>
> - See frequent informal reviews as opportunities to coach and develop.
> - Learn that communicating expectations is your responsibility, especially in a culturally diverse workplace.
> - Practice using performance evelution as a positive tool for increased productivity.

PERFORMANCE EVALUATION AS A TOOL

After you have the people you need and have worked on your own skills for managing successfully, building teams, and valuing the unique skills of each contributor, there comes a time to evaluate performance. Performance evelutions are often dreaded by all parties involved. However, you can be very positive and proactive.

In a diverse workplace, performance evaluations also provide an opportunity to learn, discuss obstacles and successes, and map ways to improve communication and productivity.

The following situation describes a setting and both parties' frames of mind. Included are two roles you can read on your own or role-play in a group.

"No Matter How Hard I Try"

GWEN COOKE

Annual evaluations always aroused mixed feelings in Gwen Cooke. On one hand they provided an opportunity to discuss progress and set goals. On the other hand, these annual performance appraisals had an atmosphere of midterm exams with raises or rewards taking the place of grades. There was always a certain amount of tension on both sides.

8

And now Ralph Tyler was about to arrive for his performance evaluation. He did adequate work but not spectacular. And recently he had been complaining to others that his being African-American was the cause for his not getting the really interesting assignments and more rapid promotion.

RALPH TYLER

Ralph Tyler's annual evaluations over the last two years hadn't resulted in promotions or high-visibility assignments. He was certain that being African-American was the reason he was not getting more rapid promotion or the really interesting assignments.

As he walked to Gwen's office, Ralph reflected, Gwen checks my work more than that of the nonblacks around here. She doesn't seem to have any confidence in my ability. Well, in just a few moments I'm going to take this chance to challenge her—*'No matter how hard I try*, you're passing me over for good assignments and promotions.' ■

1. How would you assess this situation?

_____

_____

2. Recognizing that the tone of the meeting is charged, what should Gwen do?

_____

_____

3. How would you respond if you were in Gwen's position?

_____

_____

4. How would you respond if you were in Ralph's position?

_____

_____

Points to Consider

Both Gwen and Ralph would benefit by:

- Reviews to improve morale, communication, and the quality of work.
- Frequent informal reviews for coaching and mentoring.

Gwen could better help Ralph by:

- Explaining the purpose and opportunities of the performance appraisal.
- Viewing the appraisal as a developmental tool.
- Discussing cultural and stylistic differences in accomplishing tasks.
- Offering help and access to information and networks.
- Using criticism of past performance, if needed, as a springboard for a jointly formulated action plan for improved performance.

Ralph would benefit by:

- Seizing every appropriate opportunity to ask for explanations of the organization's expectations.
- Using criticism of past performance as a springboard to ask for a jointly-formulated action plan for improved performance.
- Realizing that he may be trying hard, but his definition of good work and methods may not be the same as others' criteria and by not missing the opportunity to ask Gwen what her criteria are.
- Asking for help and access to information and networks.

8

Chapter 8 Checkpoints

✓ Realize that your employees' definitions of good work and methods may not be the same as yours.

✓ Ask employees how they assess their own efforts.

✓ Clearly tell employees your expectations and those of the organization.

✓ Coach employees on how to go about meeting those expectations.

9 | Conflict Resolution

This chapter will help you to:

- See conflict as an integral part of work life.
- See conflict as the result of differing points of view.
- Learn that these differences can contribute to the innovation and effectiveness of the organization.
- Use a model to open communication toward common goals.

CONFLICT IN THE WORKPLACE

Conflict resolution provides an opportunity for improved communication and innovation within the organization. Conflict or dispute is an inevitable and integral part of workforce realities. The interaction of individual, organizational, and cultural variables presents both danger and opportunity.

What are your current methods of confict resolution?

_____

_____

_____

_____

After you write your responses, ask yourself, Where are the stumbling blocks in this framework when we're in a multicultural situation?

_____

_____

_____

_____

Also ask yourself, How can I use the advantage of cultural diversity to bring new viewpoints to this situation?

_____

_____

_____

_____

In mixed cultural groups, conflict is often the result of communication problems. In a culturally diverse group, some knowledge of other people's ways of working, negotiating, setting priorities, and making decisions is crucial to conflict resolution.

Return to the illustration of cultural filters on page 29. From your understanding of these, reflect on current conflict situations in your workplace. Is the problem conflict or communication? What can you do to improve the communication and cultural understanding within conflict situations?

_____

_____

_____

Within each situation there is the point where the organization's culture meets the individual's culture, personality, and circumstances. The diagram on page 65 is a simple graphic representation of a single encounter of those elements.

Factors to consider as you contemplate the diagram include:

- Each organization has its own organizational culture, organization's age, and levels within the organization.
- Each individual in the organization has her own configuration of elements, increasing the complexity of interaction with both the organization and other individuals in the organization.

COMMUNICATION OR CONFLICT?

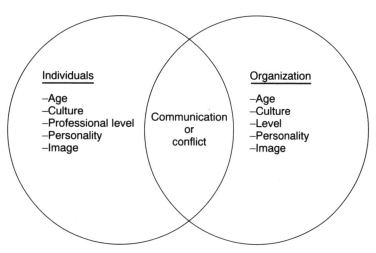

When the individual and the organization meet in *your* workplace, is the result communication or conflict?

FOCUS ON GOALS

Focusing on goals rather than on resolving conflict results in more effective leadership and management, especially within a culturally diverse environment. Rather than focus on the problem, identify the goals of the various parties concerned. Then concentrate on that goal and how to achieve it. To facilitate the process, here are five suggestions:

1. Define the Situation: What Does Each Party Want?

Prepare the environment. Often the choice of physical environment has an impact. Where are we meeting? Is it a neutral location or is it on somebody's turf, thereby creating a power imbalance?

At first, set up groups where everyone has equal status. The presence of authority figures will inhibit open communication. However, it is important at some point to have a person of authority and leadership within the organization express support and commitment for the interaction.

2. Focus on Finding a Common Goal among the Parties

What would an ideal working relationship look like?

Some coaching may be necessary to find this common goal. If skills in active listening or summarizing are lacking, use skill-building exercises in these areas. This practice time can also increase trust and respect.

If there are particularly sensitive issues, have people with various points of view present to avoid a two-sided face-off. This can dilute potential hostilities.

3. Explore Ways to Meet a Common Goal

For some cultures, negotiation or bargaining is a natural part of working together. If the conflict is between different cultural groups, include some education about how other groups communicate and prioritize. This may be done in separate sessions or within the larger group.

If an impasse occurs, take a break, use humor, invite all participants to talk about what results they want, or consider breaking into smaller groups and then coming back together.

4. All Parties Commit to a Plan of Action Focused on the Goal

What actions are you going to take to move from where you are to where you want to be? Have a definite project or next step in mind in situations where working more productively can begin immediately. It may be a small step, a fun project, or some skill training/practice. Include follow-up checkpoints in the plan of action.

5. Focus on the Common Goal Rather Than on the Hostilities and/or Differences

Part of the session or plan of action may include gathering information about the groups or individuals involved in the perceived conflict.

For current conflict situations in your workplace, keep a journal of your results as you practice this model:

_____
_____
_____
_____

9

Chapter 9 Checkpoints

✓ Conflict resolution is an opportunity for improved communication and creative innovation within the organization.

✓ Rather than focus on the problem, identify goals of the parties concerned.

✓ Concentrate on a goal and how to achieve it.

10 | Where Is Your Organization?

This chapter will help you to:

- Prepare a cultural organizational assessment.
- Learn that a cultural audit includes both subjective and objective data.
- Begin to make valuing diversity part of your organizational culture.

ORGANIZATIONAL ASSESSMENT

Have you assessed your organizational culture and the behaviors that sustain it? If so, what are they?

_____

_____

_____

Just as you did a self-assessment at the beginning of this book, you can also do an assessment of your organization. Such an assessment, often called a *cultural audit*, helps you and everyone in your organization better understand where your organization stands in relation to valuing diversity.

How would this assessment benefit your organization?

_____

_____

_____

Perhaps you mentioned that doing a cultural audit can bring to light things that no one had previously considered. The results can highlight areas that need improvement, or they may be cause to celebrate that you *are* doing a good job.

Cultural Audit of Your Organization

A cultural audit should have two parts: subjective and objective.

Subjective.   The subjective part of your audit should include:

- How people feel about working in the organization.
- What their perceptions are about the organization and their potential in it.
- What do they think they are doing to create an environment of valuing diversity.

Some Sample Questions

- Do you feel your ideas and views are listened to?
- What are you doing to create an environment of valuing diversity?
- What else would you do to create an environment of valuing diversity?

Objective.   The objective part of your audit should include:

- Hard data on the level of women and minorities in the organization.
- Frequency of promotions.
- What the measurable results are of mentoring programs and training.

10

You can use these points to begin to create a cultural audit in your organization. Talk about it with others to decide on what scale you can launch a cultural assessment of your organization, division, or department. The audit can have varying degress of formality. Use the informal assessment that follows to start brainstorming.

Organization Assessment

The shift in organizational perspective usually moves through the following stages. Check where your organization is currently.

☐   There are plenty of people just like us who want to work here.

☐   Legal obligations require new guidelines for recruiting and hiring.

☐   There aren't very many people just like us who want to work here.

☐   What a hassle it is to deal with this new group of diverse employees.

☐   Hey, this new group of diverse employees does indeed bring talents.

☐   You know, our organization should look at more effective ways to allow these talents to flower.

☐   Our organization knows we have a competitive advantage with this diverse workforce, and we're creating our new corporate culture together.

10

Chapter 10 Checkpoints

✓ A cultural audit helps clarify where your organization stands on valuing diversity.

✓ An audit can have both subjective and objective data.

✓ An organizational assessment can have varying degrees of formality and scale.

Post-Test

Assess your current understanding of diversity in the workplace by responding to the following statements.

T/F   **1.** Cultural shifts only occur when people move from one geographic area to another.

T/F   **2.** Ethnicity is the sole determinant of a cultural group.

T/F   **3.** Cultural value spectrums vary across cultures and among individuals.

T/F   **4.** The dominant American culture is individualistic.

T/F   **5.** Materialism and spirituality cannot be measured in terms of cultural values.

T/F   **6.** Stereotypes are useful as signs that point to broad areas of shared characteristics.

T/F   **7.** White males make up a minority of the American workforce.

T/F   **8.** Mentoring always involves an older person coaching a younger colleague and works best when both people are from the same cultural background.

T/F   **9.** In all cultures, assertiveness is crucial to getting desired results.

T/F   **10.** Conflict resolution is an innate skill that can't be taught or learned.

ANSWER KEY

1. F   2. F   3. T   4. T   5. F

6. T   7. T   8. F   9. F   10. F

The Business Skills Express Series

This growing series of books addresses a broad range of key business skills and topics to meet the needs of employees, human resource departments, and training consultants.

To obtain information about these and other Business Skills Express books, please call Irwin Professional Publishing toll free at: 1-800-634-3966.

Getting and Staying Organized
ISBN   0-7863-0254-2

Total Quality Selling
ISBN   0-7863-0324-7

Business Etiquette
ISBN   0-7863-0323-9

Empowering Employees
ISBN   0-7863-0314-X

Training Skills for Supervisors
ISBN   0-7863-0313-1

Moving Meetings
ISBN   0-7863-0333-6

Multicultural Customer Service
ISBN   0-7863-0332-8